Elizabeth Cole

Our diversity
makes us stronger

To all children who have ever felt different!

This book belongs to

....

....

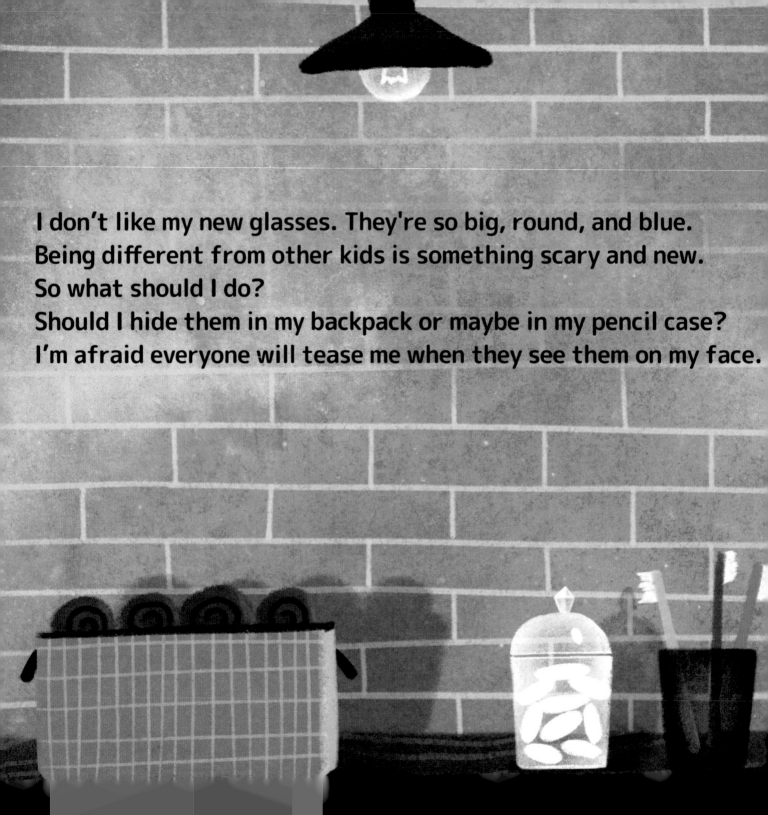

I don't like my new glasses. They're so big, round, and blue.
Being different from other kids is something scary and new.
So what should I do?
Should I hide them in my backpack or maybe in my pencil case?
I'm afraid everyone will tease me when they see them on my face.

"Hi, Nick! Look! I got new braces—they sparkle in the light.
They will make my teeth healthy and help correct my bite.
Let's go, hurry up! We don't want to be late for school.
And by the way, I like your glasses. I think they're cool."

Are they? Hmm... maybe being different isn't so bad.
Sarah has new braces and she doesn't look sad.
Diversity is of value, no matter what others may say.
I guess we are all different in some special way.

From the skin we live in—to the way we wear our hair;
From the God we pray to—to the food we eat and share.
Jason loves his skateboard and Billy rides a bike.
Some of my friends go by bus. And me? I like to hike.

"I don't like playing football, even though I'm a boy.
Ballet dancing is what brings me happiness and joy."

"Because of my accent, I sound different from you.
But, remember, for me, your language is different too."

"I can't hear very well, but it won't ruin my plans.
That's why I learned sign language by using my hands."

Wow! We are so different, and it makes us unique.
From the way we smile and walk, to the way we speak.
Fatima wears a red dot, and Milan has freckles on his face.
Without our differences, the world would be a boring place.

Every day I respect those who are different from me.
And they are as kind to my differences as they can be.

We all have different wishes. We dream different dreams.

"I love nature.
So, I will protect forests, seas, and streams

"One day, I will visit the moon
and fly to the stars."

"Maybe you will heal people,
but I'm going to heal cars."

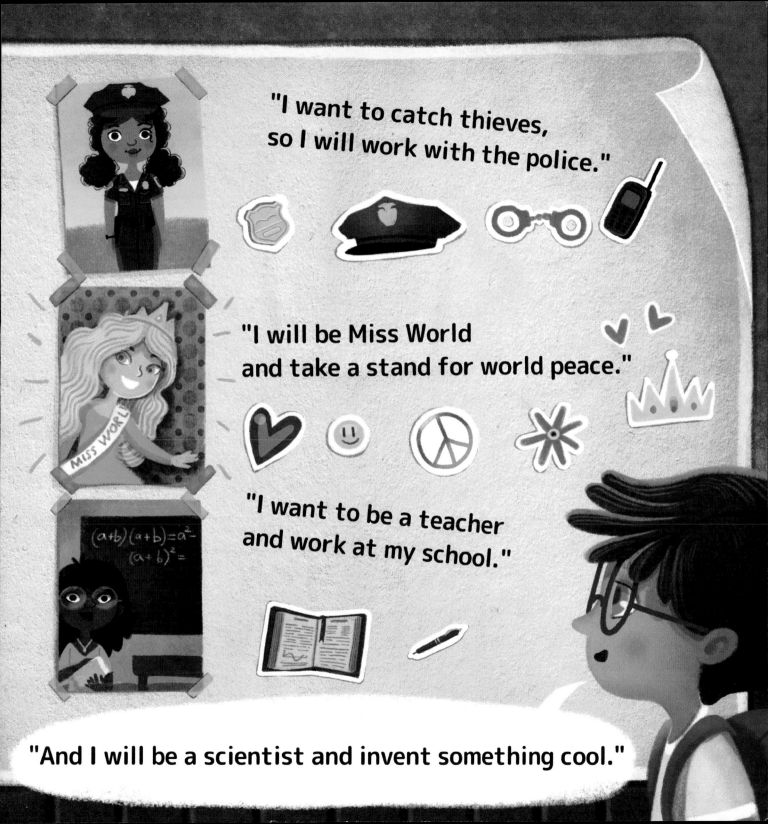

What also makes us different is how we feel.
With the same situation, we differently deal.
"I don't like to wait in line. It makes me upset.
I'm feeling restless and I'm covered in sweat."

"I am very patient. I can stay here all day long."
"I can enjoy the bright sun and sing a happy song."
"I like to wait with Lily, who always wears different hats.
We like to gossip a bit and have fun with our chats."

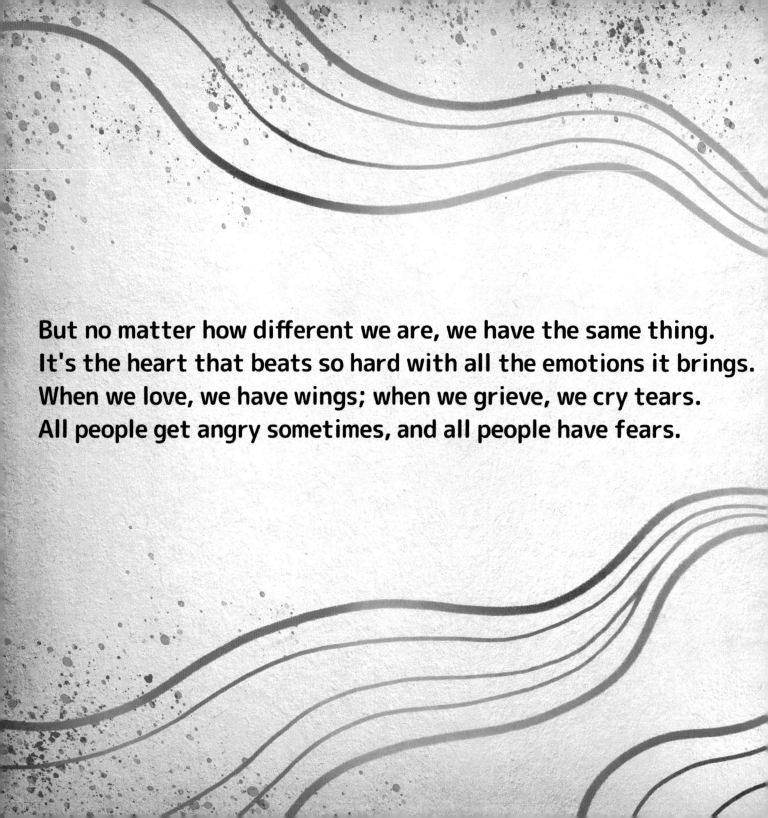

But no matter how different we are, we have the same thing.
It's the heart that beats so hard with all the emotions it brings.
When we love, we have wings; when we grieve, we cry tears.
All people get angry sometimes, and all people have fears.

And when we are scared or cry the saddest tears,
our family will drive away all sorrows and fears.
Some will find refuge in their mom's warm hugs.
Some will call their dad to fight the yucky bugs.

Some will read the Quran with bliss upon his face.
And for some, the Bible will be the peaceful place.
For those without parents, a friend will be the one
To bring a smile, a giggle, and a day full of fun.

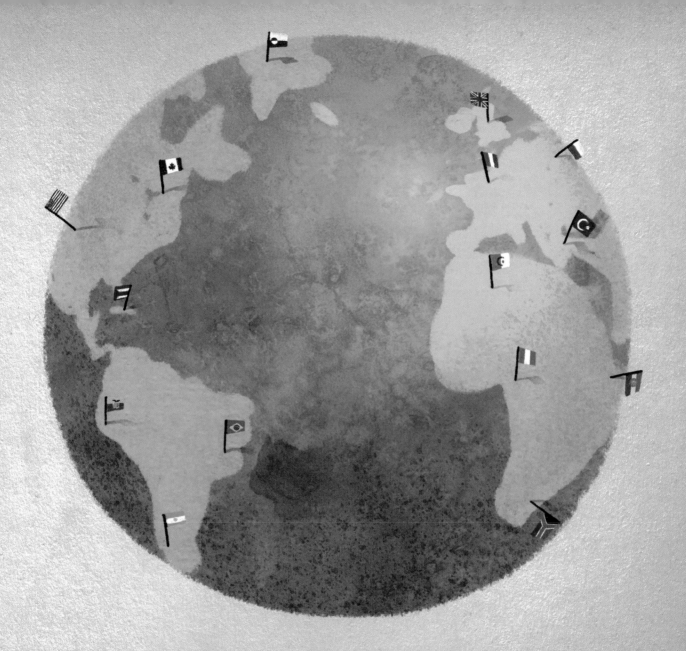

So, whether our skin is yellow, brown, black, or white,
Or our personality is shy, chatty, naughty, or polite,
And our hair is brown, blonde, braided, or curled,
All of our differences are welcome in this world.

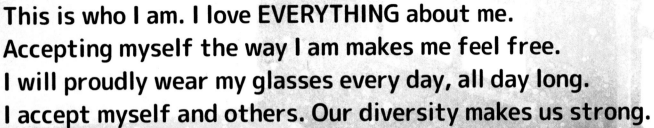

This is who I am. I love EVERYTHING about me.
Accepting myself the way I am makes me feel free.
I will proudly wear my glasses every day, all day long.
I accept myself and others. Our diversity makes us strong.

"DIVERSITY IS NOT ABOUT HOW WE DIFFER.
DIVERSITY IS ABOUT EMBRACING ONE ANOTHER'S UNIQUENESS".
-OLA JOSEPH

Please go here to get your bonus coloring page for **FREE**

Dear Reader,

Thank you for purchasing my book!
This is the fourth story from the series "World of Kids Emotions". It is aimed at teaching children the importance of diversity, helping them to accept themselves and others as well as celebrating all of our beautiful differences.

I received lots of positive comments about my first three books and I hope you enjoyed this one too! As always, a special gratitude for my young readers, your feedbacks and kindness are of utmost importance and inspire me all the time!

I am very much motivated to continue Nick's adventures! So, what kind of topic would you like to see in my next book? Please, feel free to send me your all and any thoughts and ideas.

I'm so excited to hear back from you! You can write me at elizabethcole.author@gmail.com or visit www.ecole-author.com.

I would also greatly appreciate it if you could review my book.
Here is the link to "Our diversity makes us stronger" on Amazon:

Your input means a lot to me!

With love,
Elizabeth Cole

Made in the USA
Middletown, DE
16 November 2021